LET'S COLLECT DEVON POTTERY

CONTENTS:

THE SCANDY PATTERN

"Spots and streaks and twiddles, and the peacock's feather design…" – that was how Mr. Marsland, one of the potters in Eden Phillpott's novel *'Brunel's Tower'* described a decoration he was applying to a pot. The Watcombe Pottery catalogues called it 'scando', whilst some of the old potters said 'scandee'. Dealers today describe it as 'Prince of Wales feathers' or 'art nouveau' (often an all encompassing term used to denote anything with scrolls). But, to Torquay pottery collectors it is known simply as 'the scandy pattern'.

Of all the mottoware patterns, scandy was one of the earliest and dates from the early 1890's. It has its origins in Scandinavian rosemaling and was most probably brought to Aller Vale via woodworking classes at the Cottage Art Schools in Kingskerswell, Abbotskerswell and Coffinswell. In the summer of 1889 Mr Albert Searley, one of the teachers at the Cottage Art Schools, went to Nääs, Sweden, where he qualified as a teacher of Slöjd; this was a method based on woodcarving. On his return to Devon the skills he had learned were applied to the Cottage Art Schools – according to the *Torquay Directory and South Devon Journal* of 13th November 1889 *"the first attempt at a village Slöjd School in England"*. Evidence of the influence of Scandinavian designs can be seen in woodcarvings executed by W. G. Howard (an apprentice at Aller Vale) and in the development of pottery designs, especially the scandy pattern.

Colour photo opposite:

Top row: Aller Vale scandies, left to right: Jug, 12cms (4.75") tall, c. 1910, inscribed: *"O' a little tak a little, When there's nocht tak 'a"*; plate, c. 1905, *"He may do what he will, That will do what he can"*; two handled plant pot, c. 1900, *"For every evil under the sun, There is a remedy or there is none, If there be one try and find it, If there be none never mind it"*; hot water jug, c. 1915, *"Never put off til tomorrow, What can be done today"*.
Notice that these scandies all have a kidney shaped motif on the outer scrolls copying the rosemaling design.

Middle row: More Aller Vale scandies, left to right: Jug, c. 1903, made of white clay with dark green slip ground, inscribed: *"If at first you don't succeed, try again"*; plate, 18 cms (7") diameter, c. 1908, *"The friends thou hast and their adoption tried, Grapple them to thy heart with hooks of steel"* (quotation from Shakespeare's Hamlet); candlestick, c. 1903, white clay and khaki slip background *"A safe conscience makes a sound sleep"*; bowl, 1890's, no motto.

Bottom row: Longpark scandies from the 1920's and 30's: teapot, 15.5 cms (6") tall overall, *"Du'ee have a cup o tay"*; jug and vase both have the same motto: *"Hear all. See all. Say nothing."*

2

Below is a simplified drawing of a door panel from Donstad in Morgetal, Norway, which was painted in 1850 by Knut Mevasstaul. The elements of the scandy pattern can clearly be seen with a central motif which curves upwards surmounted by fronds sweeping out on either side.

The scandy patterns decorated by the Torquay potters varied enormously as the photographs show. Aller Vale was the first pottery to produce them and early examples are often very complex with as many as 15 central fronds, whilst later (1930's) small pots may have only three. It required considerable skill to produce an even and symmetrical design as several modern potters have found when asked to copy the design.

Mr. Marsland, Eden Phillpott's decorator, described his job: *"seven colours go to each piece, and there are sixty touches of the brush upon each piece ... sometimes on my good days ... I'll do five and twenty to thirty dozen pieces as this in a day. That's eighteen thousand touches and streaks of colour in eight hours."* Although Brunel's Tower is a novel, Phillpotts carefully researched his subject, and many other descriptions of patterns are accurate so it can be assumed this is too. Such an elaborate decoration was time consuming even for the most skilled decorators and this no doubt explains why it went out of production after World War II.

By 1903 Watcombe and Hart and Moist were producing the scandy pattern, followed shortly afterwards by the newly formed Longpark

Photograph opposite: Top, left: Aller Vale tyg with very unusual central motif ; **right:** Aller Vale jam pot, c. 1905, the central motif has been 'borrowed' from the Isnik tulip pattern. **Middle, left:** Watcombe model of a Cornish pasty, 1930's; **right:** Aller Vale watering jug in the form of a cockerel, early elaborate scandy c. 1890. **Bottom, left:** model of an iron, made by the Torquay Pottery Company to advertise Dymchurch Holiday Camp, c. 1930; **right:** Watcombe jug: from the front it has a very ordinary scandy, but turn it round to see this delightful model of a mouse at the base and the motto *"You can't catch me Percy"*, c. 1912.

A Cornish Pasty

The Dymchurch
Holiday camp!

The world is full of rubs

cant catch
me –
Percy –

Pottery and the Torquay Pottery Company. In the 1920's the design was used by Daison, Devon Tors, Plymouth Gas Fired Pottery, and Barton. The scandy pattern was also taken to the Crown Dorset Art Pottery at Poole by Charles Collard, and some other potteries also copied it – examples are Powell Buckley, Wardle, and Salopian.

Scandies were usually done in several colours of slips – greens, browns and blues on a cream background are most common. However, Aller Vale did some on a blue, green or pink background – these were often over a white clay body so the pale sgraffito lettering shows through the dark background. Watcombe, rarely, used a blue background. Some scandy patterns had an amber glaze which gives a warm glow to the pot – this has been seen on pots made by Aller Vale, Watcombe and Hart and Moist, although possibly others will turn up.

Many collectors like to know the attribution of unmarked pots and there are some distinguishing features with different types of scandy. For instance, if a scandy has a tall pointed middle frond it is almost certainly from the Hart and Moist Pottery. However, not all Hart and Moist scandies are like this as some have more conventional decorations. The style of lettering, deeply cut end 'toes' on handles of pots, and gritty clay will all help to confirm identification. A pot decorated with a very thin and spindly scandy may well have originated from Barton Pottery, although these are quite rare. Daison scandies are also rare and can be distinguished by the bright blue slip and 'minimalist' neat decoration (maybe a blue dot border but not much else!). However, the Devon Tors Pottery at Bovey Tracey also used a very bright blue, which they called lapis lazuli, but Devon Tors pots are usually more elaborately decorated and have a 'greasy' base.

The best way to gain experience in identification is to look at lots of pots!! Go to pottery meetings and share your love of pots with like minded people. The scandy pattern has more variations than most other decorations so there's always something new popping up to enjoy.

Photographs opposite: Hints for identifying unmarked pots:

Top: Hart and Moist jug. Note the long pointed middle frond which is typically Hart and Moist. The irregular lettering, often sloping backwards, is also typical of Hart and Moist.
Middle: Longpark scent bottle, with asymmetrical 'rosemaling' scandy, the lettering has been done with a broad flat tool, which is typical of Longpark Pottery.
Bottom: Puzzle jug made by Aller Vale. This is from the late period, c. 1918, and is virtually identical to Watcombe of the same period. The lettering is typical of both potteries too. Note the humorous touch – the decorator has put a face on the 'tadpole' motif!

The drawing of the Norwegian panel is taken from 'Rose Painting in Norway' by Randi Asker, published by Dreyer in 1990. Thanks to Anne Beaufoy for this information.

LEMON & CRUTE Butterfly decorated 'Souvenir Ware'

by John Howell

My wife, Jan, and I are interested in British Ceramics generally – from the eighteenth century to the present day. Our interest in the Torquay potteries came about mainly through Jan, some thirty years ago. Our collection of Torquay pots is relatively small by Torquay standards and neither of us can claim to be experts in this branch of ceramics. About twenty years ago Jan developed a liking for Lemon & Crute pieces decorated with a streaky mauve background on which is painted a very stylised flag iris with a prominent butterfly, not to be confused with unmarked Longpark butterflies.

We now have 32 of these butterfly-decorated pieces, most of which are quite small, from 2" to 4.5" tall. Anything above 8" is unusual with butterfly decoration. Few of the butterflies can be recognised as of a particular species and many are poorly executed while others are very delicately painted. The background colour can vary from the usual pinkish mauve to anything between a distinct reddish tone to a really pale pink. Pieces also occur with a definite lavender background varying to a pale grey with only a hint of blue.

Lemon & Crute wares of any period are rarely painted with a motto but some of the smaller butterfly pieces are inscribed in black under the glaze with *"A Present from ..."*, hence my title, 'Souvenir Ware'. Those in our collection are mostly from towns on or near the south coast: Margate, Folkestone, Hastings, Waterlooville, Ventnor (Isle of Wight) and Poole. Two 'strays' are from Blackpool and Felixstowe.

I think it is fair to say that the majority of the butterfly pieces are from the early period of the factory's output, perhaps about 1918 to 1923.

Photographs opposite: Top row, left to right: *'A Present from Waterlooville'*, 10cms (3.75") tall, shape 15; *'A Present from Poole'*, no shape number; *'A Present from Blackpool'*, 10cms (4"), shape 44; *'From Ventnor'*, shape 463; *'A Present from Hastings'*, shape 574.
Middle row, left to right: *'A Present from Folkestone'*, shape 199; *'A Present from Margate'*, 18cms (7.25"), shape 153; *'A Present from Hastings'*, shape 199.
Bottom row – these pots demonstrate that the incised numbers refer to the shape of the pot, regardless of size: left to right: heather vase, 15cms (6"), shape 153 – compare with the vase in centre of the middle row; vase with bird, 19.5cms (7.75"), shape 44 – compare with the vase in the middle of the top row; two butterfly vases, the one on the left is 15.4cms tall, the one on the right is 11.5cms yet both are incised with shape number 265.

Mostly they have unglazed bases usually incised with a number, almost certainly to indicate the shape of the piece. Strangely, some of the shape numbers, although incised on an unglazed base, themselves contain some glaze. Some later pieces have glazed-over bases, sometimes showing the shape number through the glaze.

Looking at these shape numbers, we see that they have been allocated to indicate the shape but not the size of the piece. In the colour photo, the pots in the bottom row are of different size to those in the rows above but with the same shape numbers. For instance, the heather vase on the bottom row (left) is 15cms (6") tall, and the tall butterfly vase in the row above is 18.4cms (7.25") yet both are incised with the same shape number '153'.

Turning back to the souvenir pieces, all of ours have unglazed bases and 7 out of 8 have shape numbers. The hand-painted inscriptions, *"A Present from ..."* etc., are fairly constant and could well be by the same hand. Also, it is worth noting that we have seen no other patterns with similar inscriptions.

Jan and I would be most interested to hear any comments on what I have called 'Souvenir wares' – other towns or other patterns, etc. Also we wonder if it might be worth trying to form a 'Shapes Catalogue' with the help of others with similar interests.

Photographs opposite show the reverse of the first two rows of the colour pictures. The bottom picture shows the base of two pots: Left: incised *'Lemon & Crute, Torquay, 1920';* **right:** *'253'.*

CHARLES COLLARD – West Country potter

In 2004 Newton Abbot Town Museum mounted an exhibition on the work of Charles Collard (1874-1969). A booklet was produced to accompany the exhibition; the book gives information about Collard's life as a potter, from apprenticeship at Aller Vale, through his brief periods at Watcombe, Longpark, and Hart and Moist, before founding his own potteries at Poole (the Crown Dorset Art Pottery) and Honiton. There are photos of all 140 exhibits. This is a valuable reference book and copies can still be obtained from Newton Abbot Town Museum, 2a St. Paul's Road, Newton Abbot, Devon TQ12 2HP; the cost is £5 – please make cheques payable to Newton Abbot Town Council.

SLEUTHING IN AGATHA CHRISTIE COUNTRY

Easter 1925 Commemorative Trays Shrouded in Mystery

by Cynthia Holt

To be a natural-born nosey Parker is at once a most wonderful and a terrible thing. This dichotomy must have been abundantly appreciated by one of Torquay's most illustrious daughters, christened Agatha Mary Clarissa Miller, later to assume a prominent place on the literary world stage as Dame Agatha Christie. Were she alive today, Dame Agatha's expertise might have been sought to help solve one of Torquay pottery's more baffling mysteries surrounding a special issue tray. When several contemporary gumshoes decided to don their skulking caps and go in search of the answer to a puzzle now 80 years old, it was thought that perhaps the most intriguing way to approach the project might be as if attempting to solve a "cold case" murder mystery. The leads at the outset were few, and consisted of only the following:

The **"body"** of evidence was present in the form of three commemorative Watcombe faience trays. The names of the **"suspects"** were clearly identified in neat and precise hand on each of the trays, and consisted of "M. A. John", "Mag and Walter", and "Rella, William and Peggy". The **"place"** of the event in question was most certainly Cockington, Torquay, for two of the three trays bore a depiction of Cockington Church, whilst the third illustrated the familiar scene of the Forge. The **"time"**, also indelibly applied in black ink under-glaze, was Easter 1925. It remained to be seen if April 12th, the actual date of Easter in that calendar year, had any direct bearing on the case.

The question which burned was what specific event had brought the above-named individuals to Cockington at that particular time, and was so significant as to warrant the commissioning of personalised commemorative trays to mark the occasion?

The first two bodies of evidence had been discovered quite some time ago by Chief Inspector V. Brisco. Employing the razor sharp instincts which have served her well in tracking Watcombe fugitives far and wide, Investigator Brisco managed to capture both "M. A. John" and "Mag and Walter" in one fell swoop. She noted that, in all her many years of intensive investigative reporting, she had not seen or heard of any similar trays or other pieces of Torquay pottery commemorating Easter 1925, or indeed, Easter in any other particular year. Inspector Brisco chose to retain "M. A. John" in protective custody, but released "Mag and Walter" to another facility. They are presently being held by Margaret and Peter Sloman, owners of a popular gathering place for pottery folk in the Herts. and Essex area.

Rookie Detective C. Holt had stumbled across the third body of evidence whilst cruising the aisles of that oft-frequented scene of financial crimes – ebay. She had fended off the determined efforts of several protagonists to rescue "Rella, William and Peggy" from a remote location in South Wales, despite the fact that the amount of ransom required was substantial. It was subsequently learned that the proprietor of the site, operating under the alias of *ladydicollects*, had been engaged to clear the estate of the late Peggy and the latter's husband. *Ladydi* was subjected to a thorough interrogation following the successful completion of the ransom, which revealed the following pieces of information:

Peggy had come from a well-to-do family and had been highly educated. She had gone on to become a pharmacist, quite an unusual choice for a woman of her time and class, and had married "Idris" in 1936. Idris was a well-educated man in his own right, and as an engineer had possessed by all accounts a brilliant mind. At the time of their marriage, Peggy's father had purchased a beautiful home for them in the Llanelli area of Carmarthenshire, which was popularly known by the name of "The Castle House". Peggy and Idris were to have no children.

Peggy died approximately 13 years ago, and in the autumn of 2002, Idris suffered a serious automobile accident. It was at that time that *ladydi*, in light of her former friendship with Peggy, was called to assist in clearing the estate. In the process of sifting through the apparently myriad number of goods, Peggy's commemorative tray was discovered. When questioned about the tray by *ladydi's* husband, the hospitalised Idris had responded that he could recall nothing regarding the personal history of the tray, but only that Peggy had seemed to love it and that it had always been in the house. *Ladydi* recollected that The Castle House was a fascination, a living piece of history, and from all outward appearances had gone undisturbed from the time Peggy and Idris had established residency. The only glimmer of a clue which twinkled amidst all of the treasures in Peggy and Idris' stronghold was that of a silver frame, which contained the photograph of a woman whom *ladydi* thought might possibly have been a relative of Peggy. Inscribed on the frame was the dedication "Mr and Mrs Walter Williams". Was the unidentified woman in the picture Mag, wife of Walter?

Having exhausted our source of first-hand witness information, attention was then directed towards possible documentation of the event through various periodicals. To this end, Inspector Brisco paid a visit to the British Newspaper Library in London to comb past issues of Torquay newspapers in hope of spotting an article or advert dealing with a special happening at Easter 1925 in Cockington. Nothing of substance appeared. She then decided to write to the Vicar of Cockington church pleading our case, with the further hope that he might be able to provide a lead of some kind from old church records, but Inspector Brisco has failed to receive a reply.

It seemed as if fate were conspiring against the likelihood of our ever uncovering the truth as to the increasingly mysterious event which had beckoned Peggy and company to Torquay in that notable spring of 1925. In desperation, we realised that it was finally time to call up the reserves. Retired Desk Sergeant in-Charge of Classified Materials G. Vanstone was approached and briefed on the details, and his aid as a first-class case cracker was enlisted. Sergeant Vanstone was equal to the task, and immediately took leave from his current post of "Lord of the Manor" to undertake brisk foot patrol about his home district of Torquay, site of numerous successful investigations in the past.

He conducted a thorough check of several local history books; visited the Torquay Public Library and queried the librarian in the reference library, as well as the latter's retired predecessor; and called in at the Natural History Museum. Despite all of this, the only discovery worth marking was that the Great Britain hard court tennis championships had been held that year at (Torre) Abbey park in the week following Easter.

Desperation can drive one to some strange destinations. In the autumn of 2003, whilst in the heat of the hunt for clues and every lead seemed to take us round a wrong turn or up a blind alley, Inspector Brisco spotted a newspaper article which gave us a case of the spooks. An unknown Agatha Christie play had unexpectedly been discovered in a pile of unsolicited manuscripts in Calgary, Canada. The play was an adaptation of Agatha Christie's novel, *The Secret of Chimneys'*, which had

Photographs opposite:
Top: the Easter 1925 tray. This decoration is known as 'faience ware'; it consists of pigment painted views on a cream background under a clear glaze. The decoration was first advertised by Watcombe in 1905, but was soon copied by Longpark Pottery, Torquay Pottery Company, and later by Lemon and Crute. Early pieces depict rural scenes, usually between green borders, but occasionally tan; later on named views became popular, especially as souvenir ware, and also farmyard animals, and even flowers. During the 1920's borders of pink (as on the tray), yellow or blue were sometimes used.
Bottom: two Watcombe jugs done in faience style with rural scenes, c.1914.

had been written in **1925.** Was this a clue? Andrew Sholl, spokesperson for Agatha Christie, Ltd., was quoted as saying, *"We should never underestimate her capacity to surprise, even beyond the grave".*

At times, the work of a private investigator is a dual lesson in frustration and humility. Despite our most earnest efforts, we seem to have arrived at a place which harbours more questions than answers concerning the enigmatic Easter 1925 trays. However, through process of elimination we have managed to arrive at the conclusion that the occasion which precipitated their issue must have been that of a personal rather than an official nature, and that M. A. John, Mag and Walter, and Rella, William and Peggy all knew each other. The very fact that two of the trays had been purchased as a set implies that they had been kept together over the course of the years, or at least united at some point in time by individuals who were somehow "connected". Bill Brisco, long-time partner of the Chief Investigator, is convinced that the occasion centred around the church and has suggested the possibility of a Confirmation, which is popular at Easter, or a wedding.

As a sad post-script to the story, it was learned that Idris passed away at age 92 in the late fall of 2003, severing yet another link to Peggy and the past life of the tray. It rests now, silent and full of secrets, in a place of honour on a large display cabinet in my study. It has become one of my most cherished pottery possessions, and I am deeply grateful to have had the good fortune to join its richly endowed personal history with my own. And yet I am overwhelmed with questions whenever I gaze at it, which is often, and wonder what it was that brought Peggy and her companions to Cockington that memorable Easter so many years ago?

'COCK OF THE MORN'

Cockerels are a popular area of collecting judging by the response we've had to the article in Let's collect Devon Pottery number two. The photos opposite show two unusual examples, both showing a cock crowing at daybreak; they were both 'captured' by Joyce Stonelake.

Top: Teapot stand, 14cms (5.5") diameter, made by C. H. Brannam, c.1915. This is a moulded cockerel decorated in coloured glazes, although another example has been seen with a green glaze.

Bottom: Longpark shallow dish with deep blue slip background painted in white slip with a cock surrounded by stars and moons, c.1920.

COLLECTORS CORNER

Keith Neat loves Watcombe cottagewares

Keith Neat started collecting Watcombe mottowares with cottage decorations about thirteen years ago, although his fascination for the mottoes began long before then. Keith says *"When I was a little boy my family had some mottowares which were displayed on a high shelf which went around the room. Every year, when the pots were taken down to be washed (and one, at least, got broken!) I was fascinated by the sayings written on them. One which particularly amused me was 'The cup that cheers, but not inebriates'."*

Many years later, Keith's sister, who was then living in America, did an Arts degree and wrote a dissertation on Torquay pottery. She asked Keith to do some research, and he found her a teapot, followed by a milk jug, sugar bowl and an odd saucer. Soon he found a cup (to go with the saucer) and another teapot. By then Keith was hooked! He kept all the pots and has added to them, so he now has over 600 pots.

Keith soon found out there were other people just as 'potty' as him. He joined a pottery society and well remembers the first meeting he attended at Farnham, Surrey, in 1993: *"I couldn't believe my eyes – there were so many Torquay pots on show and for sale. I bought four pots – a coffee pot, a hot water jug, a 1476 shaped milk jug and a giant sized cup."*

Keith likes the pottery because it is hand made – he likes the individuality, and the colours of brown, tan and greens. He decided to stick to Watcombe cottages because *"I like their cottages the best and they made the widest range of items with this decoration."* Keith's aim is to have an example of every shape and size that was made – he has copies of old Watcombe catalogues so he knows what was made, *"but"*, he says, *"sometimes something completely different comes up, possibly a special commission or 'one-off' – that's part of the fun of collecting."*

Keith's collecting has also given him another hobby – making replacement lids. He bought a lidless teapot and, knowing how difficult it is to find a correct lid that fits, decided to make a lid. It turned out well, so well that other collectors began asking him to make lids for their lidless pots too.

Photograph opposite shows Keith beside his main cabinets with his mottoware collection. Keith is holding a dressing table tray with the *'Don't look for flaws...'* motto.

Does Keith have a favourite motto? He says *"I like the friendship mottoes, and also the sunshine mottoes, such as:*

The sun is always shining
Behind the darkest clouds

Keith did pick out one motto as a special favourite:

Don't look for flaws as you go through life
And even if you find them
It is wise and kind to be somewhat blind
And look for the virtues behind them.

Keith says this sums up life – but also the pots!

Can you help Keith?

He has a candlestick inscribed *'Klaarsvakie kom Aan'..* Is this Africaans – and what does it mean?

Keith has a vase with the inscription *'Greetings from Papakura'* – where is Papakura? Sounds like a New Zealand place name.

Keith is looking for porridge tureens – they were made in three sizes (6", 7.5" and 9" diameter) but he has never seen one with a cottage decoration. And Keith is also looking for vases 12" tall, or more; he says vases are rare.

Contact Keith on lidmaster@ntlworld.com - or write to the address at the front of this booklet.

Photographs opposite show some of Keith's pots:

Top: Left, muffin dish, 13cms (5") tall, with the motto: *'Du'ee have zum muffins'*. Keith says he bought this because it has an inner rim like one of the old cheese dishes.
Right: biscuit barrel, 13.5cms tall to top of knob, inscribed: *'Help yourself to biscuits'*.
Middle: left to right: vase, 20cms (8") tall, with the motto: *Think not of tomorrow's child of the king, Leave them in His hand, Do the next thing'.*; Jug, 25.5cms (10") tall, motto: *'May your joys be as deep as the ocean, Your sorrows as light as it's foam'*. Pot-pourri vase, 15cms (6") tall, motto: *'The sun is always shining, Behind the darkest clouds'*.
Bottom: The smallest mini jug is just 5cms (2") tall and is inscribed *'Speak little, Speak well'*; the other items are all from Broadway and have thatched roofs which curve over the dormer windows; Keith says they are more elaborate, being decorated using 8 colours. The small jug on the left is inscribed *'Take a little cream'*; the teapot (sporting one of Keith's lids) is 14cms (5.5") tall and has the motto *Drown your sorrows in a cup of tea*; the barrel shaped jug on the right is 11.5cms (4.5") tall and has the motto *Kind words are the music of the world*.

20

BIRD JUG AND DISH by Stuart Bass

Nigel and Alison Wildsmith from Yorkshire have sent us photos of two pots from their collection – both prompted by articles in Let's Collect Devon Pottery.

On the left is a bird jug. Nigel wrote: *"I was interested in Joyce Stonelake's article on Bird Jugs in Let's Collect Devon Pottery number three and thought readers might like to see a modern version of a traditional style. This jug was made by Stuart Bass, probably in the 1980's. It's a simple bottle shaped jug with the neck moulded to form a bird's head. The wings are painted in pigments.*

And, whilst still on the subject of birds, we have a bowl with a superbly painted 'sketch' of an owl. Readers of Let's Collect Devon Pottery number two will have seen the cockerel dish decorated by Stuart Bass, and we hope you'll enjoy seeing this owl. We have a growing collection of Stuart Bass's work – he is a superb pottery artist."

Stuart Bass is semi-retired but still makes a few pots from his home in Devon. Much of his time is taken up making character pie funnels which are particularly popular with Americans.

CANDY TILES AT SANDYGATE POTTERY

In issue number three we featured the Sandygate Pottery, which was at Kingsteignton, and showed a photograph of the architectural panel which used to adorn the entrance to the works. The panel was made up of ceramic tiles painted to show the Archangel Michael slaying a dragon. This panel has been in private ownership for some time, following the closure of the Sandygate Pottery in the 1990's. Recently, one of the tiles came loose and displayed a clear backstamp 'Candy'! We had *assumed* that the tiles had been made at Sandygate (which would seem obvious), but not so. Presumably the Candy tiles were thought to be more durable as the Company specialised in architectural work. But... it just goes to prove – never make assumptions!

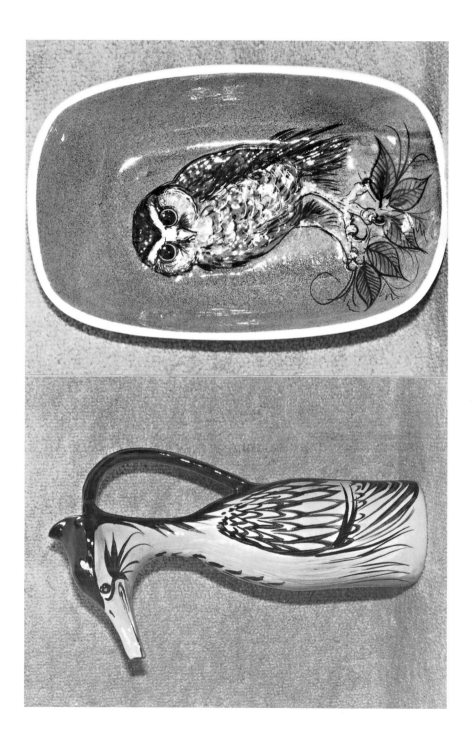

DEVONSHIRE POTTERIES Ltd.

Issues one and two of Let's Collect Devon Pottery included articles about Devonshire Potteries Ltd., which was at Bovey Tracey. Pat and Brian Adams from Dawlish, Devon, have sent us two photos of the Devonshire pottery workers and one of these is shown opposite. This photo was taken in the 1960's on a Dawlish Coaches outing. The workers are, from left to right:

Margaret Gregory (fettler); Eileen Sharp (fettler); Violet Easterbrook (fettler); Rene Weeks (maker); Gwen Barrett (fettler); Charlie Hydon (general); Evelyn ? (dipping); Don Davis (dipper); Barbara Hunt (general); Esther Weeks.

The second photo which Pat and Brian sent was unfortunately slightly out of focus so could not be reproduced. This was taken around 1970, outside the pottery, and the workers who have been identified include:

Yvonne Billings; Norma Bryant (fettler); Les Worsdale (mould maker); Beryl Stonelake (painter); Esther Weeks (head decorator); Les Manley (making); Doreen Kelly (glost); Barbara Challis (making); Gwen Barrett (making); Vivian Black (fettler); Ron Wills (pughouse); Sylvia Ayres (fettler); Mr Lewis (general manager); Shirley Fewings (making); Barbara Hunt (biscuit); Vera Tucker (painter); Pat Meardon (general).

Mr Lewis is almost certainly Leo Lewis who had previously worked for Dartmouth Pottery. We now have names of many of the workers from the early 1950's right through to the 1970's and thank all concerned for helping to build up a picture of Devonshire Potteries Ltd.

THE MUSEUM OF BARNSTAPLE AND NORTH DEVON has recently acquired the major part of Audrey Edgeler's collection of north Devon pottery, which is on display in their newly refurbished Art Pottery gallery. The pots look fantastic and are a 'must see' for all Devon pottery enthusiasts. The museum is in The Square, Barnstaple. For enquiries, phone Alison Mills on 01271 346747 – if you are travelling any distance a call is advisable as the gallery is occasionally used for other special exhibitions, which means some of the pots are temporarily removed.

EARLY BRANNAM WARES

by Virginia Brisco

The *Pottery Gazettes* provide a wealth of material for researchers interested in the Devon potteries. There are advertisements, advertising features on new ranges, notes on exhibitions and, occasionally, articles on the history of the potteries. The *Pottery Gazette* of September 1 1931 carried a feature on C. H. Brannam Ltd., including an interview between their own Reporter and Mr. Brannam; it provides a fascinating insight into the pottery.

The purpose of these articles was to inform and educate the pottery industry, but they also served to promote and publicise individual potteries, and pottery towns. On this occasion, the *Pottery Gazette* Reporter had intended, on his visit to Barnstaple, *"to visit and describe each of the two potteries"* (i.e. C. H. Brannam and William Baron, two great rivals) and he started with Baron. However, when he approached the pottery, *"we found the proprietor so busily occupied in catering for the delectation of a big coach party that it seemed perfectly hopeless for us to establish with him that personal touch without which it would have been impossible for us to write informatively of his operations. We decided, therefore, to rest content with a description of one of these potteries only..."* and moved on to Brannam's; here they were *"cordially received by Mr. C. H. Brannam"*. One up to Mr. Brannam over his rival!

Although the article in the *Pottery Gazette* dealt with the history of the pottery to 1931, it is the early part of that story which is of concern to us now. Mr. Brannam started by recounting the origins of the family pottery:

"... this was the site of a redware pottery 227 years ago (but) my father, Mr. Thomas Brannam, came here from Bideford about 90 years ago, and worked for some years as an operative potter before he decided to purchase the business. At one time the only things that were produced were ordinary, everyday, common, red household earthenware lines – nothing more. Those were very different times from now, as you may gather when I tell you that in those days a capable thrower was paid somewhere about 13s. (65 pence) a week."

Photographs opposite: Puzzle jug, pitcher and money box made in the 1870's. Puzzle jug made for Bill Brannam and his wife, inscribed: *W. J. and K. M. Brannam, EXETER, 4th January 1933*. Bill Brannam went to work in the office of the LNER railway at Exeter and his job was to persuade customers to use their routes for freight.

C. H. Brannam went on to explain that he assisted his father in *"the manufacture ot common, useful redwares"* but he was interested in 'art matters' and studied at the local art school. In 1877 Charles thought it was time his father's pottery *"explored fresh channels and attempted the manufacture of a better class of ware."* Most of the *"common useful redwares"* would have been purely domestic – drainpipes, plant pots, milk pans, pitchers etc. However, a few decorated wares were produced and three examples of this type of ware are shown in the photographs. They were owned by the late William J. (Bill) Brannam whom I first met in 1989.

Bill Brannam was born c.1904 at 37 Pilton Street, Barnstaple, the great grandson of James Brannam, cousin to Charles Hubert Brannam. Charles' father, Thomas Backway Brannam, was the elder brother of James' father, also called James. James (junior) was a plumber and had a plumbing/sanitary ware shop in Barnstaple – he did all the plumbing work for the pottery and also for the many cottages which Charles bought, so the cousins were close.

The puzzle jug, pitcher and money box shown in the photo were made in the early 1870's. The puzzle jug is inscribed under the handle *'Waste not, want not, August 20 1871'*. The money box is inscribed *'Be wise and live to the Lord April 24 164'*. The pitcher does not have an inscription. The question is – who made these pots, and where?

Bill Brannam told me he believed the pots to have been made at Thomas Backway Brannam's Litchdon Street pottery. Bill's son, Patrick Brannam, has done a lot of research into his ancestors and he believes the pots were made by his great great grandfather, James Brannam (senior) – this James was listed in various documents (Census Returns etc.) as a potter, although at the Great Exhibition of 1851 he was awarded a bronze medal for, amongst other things, *"an improved invention for water closets"* – a trade his son took up. If the pots *were* made by James Brannam, *where* did he make them? Did he work for his younger brother, Thomas, or did he run a separate pottery? If he ran another pottery, where was it? My guess is that James (by the 1870's he was in his late 60's) worked for Thomas.

What these pots do show us is the type of wares being made by the Brannam family in the early 1870's. They are crudely decorated and demonstrate why the 'art-educated' Charles Hubert thought his father's pottery should *"attempt the manufacture of a better class of ware"*!

Patrick Brannam's discussion paper, *'James Brannam and a minor mystery'* appeared in the Northern Ceramic Society Newsletter no. 100, published December 1995.

BUTTERFLIES – and other winged insects

by Virginia Brisco

Butterflies have been one of the enduring motifs for artists (and writers) for centuries so it is not surprising that the Devon potters used them too. Butterflies are fragile, delicate and pretty – and they evoke images of summer and freedom from cares and woes; remember carefree childhood days spent chasing butterflies?

The butterflies depicted on Devon pots are sometimes artistic copies of particular species, but more often they are stylised, with colours chosen more for their artistic merit than biological accuracy. Many butterflies could be moths, and some could be dragonflies so we have included a variety of all these winged insects to show the huge range of wares that were made.

The earliest pots made at the Watcombe Pottery in the 1870's were of unglazed terracotta, and it is during this period that butterflies first appear. The Watcombe Pottery started by making statuettes, busts and vases based on classical forms, but within a few years they broadened their range to include more modern designs. One of the designers they used was Christopher Dresser, who was inspired by Japanese styles and motifs. Dresser used butterflies a lot, especially in his work for Minton's, but also for the teapots and bottle vases he designed for Watcombe; these are hard to find nowadays, but much sought after by both Watcombe and Dresser collectors.

Princess Louise, Queen Victoria's sixth child, is credited with bringing butterflies into the Aller Vale repertoire of designs. Princess Louise was 'introduced' to Aller Vale pottery in 1885 at the Cottage Arts Association Exhibition which was held at Carlton House Terrace, in London, the home of Lord Brownlow. The following year Princess Louise visited the Aller Vale Pottery and, according to the *Torquay Directory and South Devon Journal* of 10th November 1886, *"made various practical suggestions for new effects and decorations"*. The reporter continued that she was pleased with what she saw at the pottery and *"sanctioned the naming of one of the most recent productions after herself, Princess Ware"*; however, there was no description of the design.

Almost a decade later, in February 1895, an article in the *Pottery Gazette* recalled, and elaborated on, this event: *"remarking that one style of ornament was almost a reproduction of Florentine work, she* (Princess

Louise) *said 'why not introduce some local feature, to take off the purely Italian character of the work? You have been telling me Devonshire legends and folk lore; there surely must be something that would be useful." A small blue butterfly was mentioned, the sole habitat of which, in the British Isles, is in the Start Bay district of the South Hams. "The very thing" exclaimed the Princess; and since then, this has become a feature of this particular ware, which, by the permission of HRH, then granted, is known as 'Princess Louise Ware'".*

Given that the Pottery Gazette account was nine years after the event took place the accuracy of the 'verbatim' reporting could be called into question! Princess (Louise) Ware (as we know it today) consists of an all-over floral design interspersed with butterflies – some blue, but some are yellow, pinky-buff, or even black. It is a very delicate pattern which is popular with collectors today.

In the south Devon potteries it is very rare to find pots that have been signed by the decorator, leading to endless debate amongst collectors as the 'who designed what'. One possibility for the 'Princess Ware' comes from a soap box, made and signed at Longpark Pottery by Frederick Blackler, who had previously worked at Aller Vale. The soap box has a decoration which is so like Princess Ware that it must have been done by a decorator well used to executing that pattern. Frederick Blackler made the box for personal use and the design was not used at Longpark (unless any of our readers know differently!!).

At the same time as Princess Ware was evolving, butterflies and dragonflies were being used by other Devon potteries in a variety of ways. For instance, Watcombe Pottery produced pilgrim vases and urns with finely painted butterflies amongst foliage. Sometimes these were

Photographs opposite: Top row, left to right: Aller Vale beaker, c. 1898, decorated with the Princess pattern; Watcombe vase, c. 1904, decorated in slips with a peacock butterfly amongst pussy willows and grasses; Torquay Pottery Co. jug, c. 1925, with applied butterfly and bulrushes done in pigments.
Middle row, left to right: Longpark pinched top vase, c.1925, painted in pigments with three butterflies on a streaky purple background; Torquay Pottery Co. vase with applied butterfly, c. 1928; Lemon and Crute vase, c. 1922, painted in pigments with a tortoiseshell butterfly on a streaky pink background.
Bottom row, left to right: Three Watcombe pots spanning 50 years. The vase on the right is the earliest, c. 1903, and shows a brimstone butterfly done in Japanese style with bamboo – the decoration has been outlined in sgraffito and filled in with slips; next in chronological order comes the jug on the left which is decorated in north Devon style and was made c. 1915 – the pot is made of white clay with some slip decoration of a dragonfly and leaves under a blue glaze; the tall vase is the most recent, being made in the late 1950's – it is decorated in bright 'contemporary' colours with a butterfly over a lily pond.

done in enamels on plain terracotta, other times in pigments under glaze. Many were decorated by Holland Birbeck who was especially fond of painting insects of all types.

Some Aller Vale decorators incorporated dragonflies into their flower and fruit designs. Charles Collard is known to have done this and he sometimes put flowers or fruit on the front of a pot and a dragonfly on the back. Collectors should always look at the back of a pot – there are often surprises in store! The popularity of Aller Vale's slip decorated butterflies encouraged other potteries, especially Watcombe and Longpark, to copy them – mostly they date from the period leading up to World War I.

By the 1890's moulded insect wall pockets were being produced by C. H. Brannam in north Devon as well as Aller Vale. Brannam's dragonfly wall pockets are particularly finely modelled and decorated.

The photographs show how butterfly and dragonfly patterns were adapted to suit changing fashions. In the 1920's and 30's brighter colours were used, reflecting the Art Deco Movement. Longpark Pottery and Lemon and Crute used streaky mauve or blue backgrounds with brightly painted butterflies. The Torquay Pottery Company did butterflies on a dark blue ground, and also a moulded butterfly alighting on a pot which is typically decorated with bull-rushes – not surprisingly, many of these butterflies have been damaged so collectors should check them carefully when purchasing.

After World War II slip painted butterflies continued to be used at Watcombe, on a bright turquoise background - a fashionable 'contemporary' colour of the 1950's. And, even into the 1990's, although the old Torquay potteries have long been closed, the tradition has been carried on by Gilly Jones at Scores Pottery in North Devon. These pots are charming in their own right, but some dealers are selling them as 'old mottowares' which they are not. Buyer beware.

Photograph opposite:

Top: part of a tea set which was given by Bill Howard to his brother and sister-in-law on the occasion of their marriage in 1903. This is Princess Louise ware, given the pattern code H1, and the butterflies are in buff and blue.

Bottom: Soap box, 20cms (8") wide, made and decorated by Frederick Blackler at Longpark Pottery in 1909. The similarity in style of decoration with the tea set above is obvious, although the Longpark box is painted in pigments whereas the Aller Vale pots are slip decorated.

Above: Watcombe Pottery teapot, designed by Christopher Dresser. Unglazed terracotta with transfer printed butterfly. Made c. 1880.

Left: Jug with elongated spout, 12.5cms (5") tall, decorated in pigments in a style reminiscent of 'Cantagalli' pottery; insect incorporated into the design. Attributed to Domenico Marcucci, an Italian pottery artist from Faenza who worked at Aller Vale from 1889 to c. 1897. This decoration is probably the pre-cursor of the H1 pattern.

Photographs opposite:

Top row, left: Aller Vale wallpocket, 24cms (9.5") wide, moulded as a moth and decorated with slip flowers in barbotine style – made in the 1890's. **Right:** Brannam butterfly wallpocket, back-plate 18cms (7") tall, made in 1896
Middle row, left: Brannam wallpocket, 24cms (9.5") tall, moulded to represent a dragonfly on a leaf, c. 1900; **Right:** Longpark shovel shaped butter or jam dish, decorated in pigments by Frederick Blackler in 1914.
Bottom row, left: Watcombe pilgrim flask, 20cms (8") tall, made in the 1880's; the superb painting of butterflies amongst blossom was most probably done by Holland Birbeck. **Right:** jug, decorated in slips by Gilly Jones, of Scores Pottery, in the 1990's.

THE FARMERS MARKET, LOS ANGELES

Kathy Brown, a Torquay pottery collector from Oregon, USA, was given a copy of **Let's Collect Devon Pottery number three** *by an English friend. Kathy was especially interested in the article on the Watcombe cottage-ware cream jug with the inscription: "Farmers Market, Los Angeles", and she writes:*

I did enjoy the booklet especially Cynthia Holt's story and picture of a jug on the Farmers Market. I have a dear friend, Phyllis Magee, who is manager of a family business there, called 'Magee's Kitchen'. Phyllis's mother in law, Blanche Magee, was one of the original tenants when the market was founded in 1934; Blanche retired in 1964 and Phyllis took over. At the end of 2001 Phyllis received a 'Women of Distinction' award, given by the Hollywood Chamber of Commerce, in honour of her long standing contribution to the local community.

Quite obviously, Phyllis Magee is a remarkable lady and Kathy would love to find a 'Farmers Market' jug to give to her. The jug in Cynthia's article is not for sale, but – has anyone got one they would be prepared to sell to Kathy? Her email address is kintheforest@charter.net - or you can contact us and we'll put you in touch with Kathy.

MEMORABLE MOTTO

Keith Neat has recently acquired at Watcombe plate, decorated with a cottage, with a very unusual motto:

A Cornish Pasty

Pastry rolled out like a plate
Piled with Turmut, Tates and Mate
Doubled up and baked like fate
That's a 'Cornish Pasty'

For the uninitiated, *'Turmut, Tates and Mate'* can be translated as turnips, potatoes and meat, the standard ingredients of a Cornish pasty. In poor households, there would be a lot more turnips and potatoes than meat.

"KEEP ME ON THE DRESSING TABLE"

by Virginia Brisco

Dressing table sets are popular amongst Torquay Pottery collectors, but there is some confusion over which items were included in a 'set'. The first 'confusion' to clear up is that our ancestors knew them as 'trinket sets', not dressing table sets, even though they were made to display on the dressing table. The second 'confusion' to clear up is that the items included in a 'set' varied, partly dependent on fashion, but also on the customer's own preferences.

Trinket sets became fashionable during the Victorian period and the Watcombe Pottery advertised them in their 1884 catalogue (see pages 42 and 43). In their introduction to the catalogue the Company claimed:

"We intend to produce articles of everyday use in such a manner as shall commend them to persons of the most refined and fastidious taste, while we have fixed our prices to suit persons of moderate means."

The catalogue listed three types of trinket sets – the Devon, the Maidencombe and the Cornish – each comprising six pieces: ring stand, powder box, puff box, pin tray, tray and a pomade jar. The puff box was to hold a powder puff, the pin tray was for hair pins (not hat pins), and pomade was a perfumed dressing for the hair or scalp. The Cornish set had a different shaped powder box – the set only listed five items, but presumably this is a clerical error!

The price list states that 'tapers and spills' could be added to the sets, and four shapes were shown in the catalogue; these would have been for spills to light candles yet the 'sets' do not include candlesticks, although they could be purchased separately. The trinket sets were available in different finishes – 'plain' (plain terracotta); 'damascene' (terracotta with straight or wavy ribbing milled into the terracotta); 'underglaze' (painted underglaze with various decorations) and 'impasto' (thick 'orange peel' background with slip decorated flowers, birds etc.). Although the catalogue lists such an extensive range of trinket sets they are rarely seen today – we shall be pleased to hear from readers who have one (or more!).

Moving on about thirty years to a Watcombe catalogue published c. 1914, trinket sets are shown in 'scando ware' (the scandy pattern);

these comprised 8 pieces – a tray, pair of candlesticks, pomade jar, powder jar, puff box, pin tray and a ring stand. The items are very much the same shape as in 1884 with the exception of the tray which is now rectangular with the corners cut off. The trinket sets were sold at 60/- (£3) per dozen sets wholesale price. Although none of the other decorations shown advertised 'trinket sets' it would have been possible for retailers to make up their own sets as the items were available individually. There were also many other items advertised which could be added to trinket sets, for instance, hat pin stands and hair tidies (these were for holding loose hairs cleaned out of the hairbrush before disposing of them in the dustbin).

By the late 1920's Watcombe Pottery was advertising a wide range of trinket sets, consisting of eight pieces although the pieces were not itemised (presumably the same as in the 1914 catalogue). Plain colours (blue, green and tangerine) were 72/- (£3.60) per dozen sets, scando and cottage also at 72/-, but Moorland Cottage, Kingfisher, Marine, Lake, and Windmill were dearer, at 120/- per dozen sets.

By the mid/late 1930's trinket sets were not advertised at all in the Watcombe catalogue, although the items were sold individually – possibly a consequence of the Great Depression. The same was true of a Longpark catalogue of the same period. Longpark also advertised some additional items not seen in the Watcombe catalogue, such as trinket boxes (no picture of these though) and hair pin boxes – these were shallow oval boxes with lids, which are highly sought by collectors today.

In the aftermath of World War Two fashions had changed and ladies no longer needed puff boxes and powder bowls – their powder came as a solid block to be put on with a sponge pad! Hair pin trays, ring holders and hair tidies had become redundant too – they were just 'old fashioned'! The only item from the 1884 trinket sets still being made was the pin tray, but even that was now marketed as a 'butter pat'. Times really had changed!

Photograph opposite:
Top: Longpark trinket set, unglazed terracotta decorated with blossom and leaves done in oils. Notice the glass drip tray to catch hot candle wax. These sets were made in the 1920's, although some collectors have mis-dated them to the 1890's because the decoration is more typical of that period; however Bill Howard (chief Longpark decorator) is known to have decorated many terracotta items in this style in the 1920's, and backstamps on the items confirm this date.
Middle: Scandy pattern trinket set assembled by Kathy Brown. Kathy was delighted to find the Longpark oval hair pin box shown on the front of the tray.
Bottom: Devon Tors trinket set, made in the 1930's, for Joyce, wife of Ken Bond, one of the owners of the pottery; decorated with violets on a pale beige slip background.

ISSN 1468-3091/ISBN 0 9520045 4 2

LET'S COLLECT
DEVON
POTTERY

ISSUE NUMBER FOUR

PRICE GUIDE

Editor: VIRGINIA BRISCO

LET'S COLLECT DEVON POTTERY

PRICE GUIDE TO ISSUE NUMBER FOUR – November 2005

This price guide is issued free with Let's Collect Devon Pottery issue no. 4 (ISSN 1468-3091/ISBN 0 9520045 4 2), which is published by Virginia and Bill Brisco, Inglefield, 218 Sandridge Road, St. Albans, Herts., AL1 4AL.

Over the past two to three years prices have dropped for Devon pottery – on average by about 25%, so it is definitely a buyers market. This leaflet is intended to be a price guide, not a price list, and reflects the prices at a wide range of outlets (fairs, auctions, shops) all over Britain.

General points: All prices quoted are on the basis that the pot is in perfect condition. Very minor chips or hairlines will devalue it by about 10%, more substantial damage, missing lids etc., by 30% - a pot with major damage, such as a teapot with no spout and handle, or a pot in several pieces, has very little value at all. Even if a pot has been beautifully restored it is still not perfect.

Front cover: Torquay Pottery Co. candlestick with applied butterfly, £40-£50; Aller Vale jug with H1 pattern – this jug is 9cms (3.5") tall and the pattern is very sought after by collectors, therefore it would command £55-£65; shallow tray, Longpark, about 14cms (5.5") across, very rare design, £50-£60; large Watcombe muffin dish £60-£70

Back cover: Hart and Moist plate, 20cms (8") diameter, £35-£40; Torquay pottery ring holder, ship design, £20-£25; Baron model of a monkey £45-£55.

Page 3: The Scandy pattern: top row, Aller Vale scandies, left to right: jug, 12cms tall, £20-£25; plate, £25-£30; double handled plant pot with unusual scandy £28-£32; hot water jug, £30-£35.
Middle row, Aller Vale scandies, left to right: jug, rarer because it has a dark green ground, £30-£35; plate, with motto from Shakespeare, £35-£40; candlestick, unusual khaki background, £30-£35; small bowl, unusual early scandy, £25-£30.
Bottom row, Longpark scandies from the 1920's and 30's, left to right:: teapot, 15.5cms tall, £30-£35; jug and vase £20-£25 each.

Page 5, top left, tyg with very unusual scandy, £50-£60; top right, jam pot with scandy and Isnik style central motif, £35-£40.

Middle row, left, model of a Cornish pasty – these are rarely seen and highly sought after, hence the guide price of £120-£150; right, another rare and sought after watering jug in the form of a cockerel, Aller Vale, £120-£150.

Bottom row, left: model of an iron to advertise Dymchurch holiday camp, made by the Torquay Pottery Co. £55-£65; right, Watcombe jug with applied mouse, £60-£65

Page 7: top, Hart and Moist jug, £22-£26; middle, Longpark scent bottle to advertise 'Quants Eau de Cologne', £25-£30; bottom, Aller Vale puzzle jug, £35-£40.

Page 8: Lemon and Crute butterfly souvenir wares: top row; small items such as these would be £15-£25. Middle row, left and right, £18-£20, middle £32-£38. Bottom row, left to right: vase with heather, £28-£32; tall vase with bird decoration, £32-£38; waisted vases £20-£30.

Page 15: Watcombe tray, Easter 1925, expect to pay £160-£180 for this rare item. Watcombe jugs decorated with animals, £90-£110 each.

Page 17: Cockerels: top, Brannam teapot stand, multicoloured glazes, £45-£50, monocoloured versions would command £30-£35. Bottom, Longpark shallow dish, very rare pattern, £50-£60.

Page 21: Watcombe cottagewares: top row, left, large muffin dish, £60-£70; right, biscuit barrel, £90-£120 (this straight sided version is rarer than the squat bulbous barrels). Middle row, left to right, vase, £25-£30, large jug, 25.5cms, £80-£90; pot pourri, £40-£45. Bottom row, left to right: jug and small mug, £15-£20 each; teapot, £28-£35, barrel shaped jug £25-£28.

Page 23: Stuart Bass: bird jug, £30-£35; shallow dish decorated with an owl, £18-£20.

Page 26: Early Brannam pots are rare so expect to pay £80-£100 each for the jug, puzzle jug, and money box. Monocoloured puzzle jugs from the 1930's will fetch around £35-£40, more for personalized inscriptions.

Page 30: Butterfly decorations: top row, left to right: Aller Vale beaker with H1 design £60-£80; tall Watcombe vase, £50-£60; Torquay Pottery Co. jug with applied butterfly, £28-£35.

Middle row, left to right: Longpark vase, 18cms (7") tall, £35-£40; Torquay Pottery vase, £65-£70; Lemon and Crute vase, £28-£30.
Bottom row, left to right: Watcombe pots: very rare jug in North Devon style, £55-£65; 1950's style vase, £40-£45; vase in Japanese style, rare, £50-£55.

Page 32: top: H1 pattern teaset: teapot, £160-£180; sugar bowl and jug about £50 each; cup and saucer, £100-£120. The Longpark soap dish is a 'one-off'.

Page 34: top left: Aller Vale wall pocket, £90-£110; top right, Brannam wall pocket £80-£100; middle row, left, Brannam dragon fly wall pocket, rare item, £250-£280; middle right: Longpark 'shovel' shaped jam or butter dish, very rare pattern, £70-£80; bottom left, Watcombe 'porcelain' style pilgrim flask, 20cms (8") tall, £80-£100; bottom right: Gilly Jones jug, £10-£15.

Page 35: top, Watcombe teapot, design attributed to Christopher Dresser, £50-£60; bottom: Aller Vale 'majolica' style jug £30-£35.

Page 39: Dressing table sets: top: Longpark terracotta set, 1920's, £60-£70; middle row: price guide for individual items: candlesticks, £30-£35 pair; large tray, £60-£80 (price dependent on decoration – large elaborate, or double, scandies are in this range, sparse or poorly executed scandies would be £50-£60); hat pin holder, £30-£35; hair tidy with lid, £30-£35; ring tree, £25-£30; oval hair pin box, £32-£38 (these are quite hard to find); pomade pot and powder bowl £25-£30 each. Bottom row: Devon Tors set decorated with violets £75-£80.

Page 41: Watcombe dressing table sets: top, set with fuchsia decoration, £120-£140; bottom, marine view set, £130-£140.

Page 46: Monkey business: top, left: Devonmoor ashtray, £20-£25 (these also come in brown clay and are earlier than the white clay versions – price is about the same); right, Watcombe ashtray, £60-£80 (these are also seen with a small square base, price guide £45-£55).
Middle, left to right: Hart and Moist monkey, £50-£60; Brannam inkwell, very rare item, £300-£350; Baron monkey, £45-£50.
Bottom row: Alan Young: pair of smugglers, £70-£75, single figures £30-£35. Alan Young figures do not generally command such high prices as his father, Will Young.

Page 48: Candy miniature fireplace, salesman's sample? £45-£50.

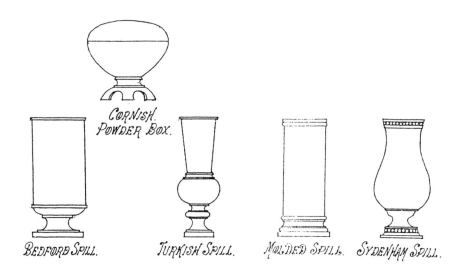

CORNISH.
POWDER BOX.

BEDFORD SPILL.   TURKISH SPILL.   MOLDED SPILL.   SYDENHAM SPILL.

From a Watcombe Catalogue, 1884: the Cornish powder box was part of the 'Cornish trinket set'. Selection of spill vases which could be added to trinket sets if desired.

THE DEVON POTTERY COLLECTORS' GROUP

The Devon Pottery Collectors' Group is an informal group for collectors and enthusiasts interested in all kinds of Devon pottery (North Devon, 'Torquay', Bovey, Honiton etc.). There are two meetings a year, in February and July, both held in Torquay; meetings open at 11am til 3.30pm although visitors can stay for as long (or as little) as they like. There are stalls selling pottery, experts on hand all day to identify and discuss pots, and two talks on various aspects of the potteries. Entry is free, there are refreshments available all day and everyone is assured of a warm welcome.

The Devon Pottery Collectors Group also promotes research into Devon potteries. The Group assisted with the Collard Exhibition at Newton Abbot Town Museum in 2004, and gave a donation to the Museum of Barnstaple and North Devon to help with the gallery refurbishment for displaying Audrey Edgeler's collection of North Devon pottery.

For more information on the Group and its activities, phone Joyce Stonelake on 01803 327277, email Virginia.Brisco@care4free.net, or write to the address at the front of this booklet.

Watcombe trinket sets: the fuchsia pattern was introduced in 1914; the Marine ware dates from c.1928.

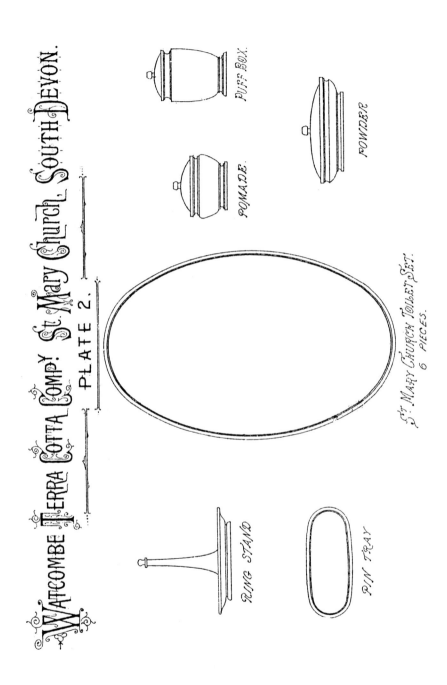

WATCOMBE TERRA COTTA COMPY. St. Mary Church, South Devon.

PLATE 2.

PUFF BOX.

POMADE.

POWDER.

RING STAND

PIN TRAY

St. Mary Church Toilet Set.
6 PIECES.

TRINKET SETS, &C.

	Plain	Damascene	Underglaze	Impasto
CORNISH TRINKET SET				
6 pieces, complete ..	4/-	6/-	10/-	14/-
Ring Stand ..	10d.			
Powder Box (plate 10)	10d.			
Puff Box ..	10d.			
Pin Tray ..	5d.			
Tray ..	1/4			

Tapers and Spills for any of the above at from 8d. to 2/6 each.

	Plain	Damascene	Underglaze	Impasto
DEVON TRINKET SET				
6 pieces, complete ..	3/-	4/6	9/-	13/-
Ring Stand ..	8d.			
Powder Box ..	8d.			
Puff Box ..	8d.			
Pin Tray ..	4d.			
Tray ..	1/-			
Pomade ..	8d.			
MAIDENCOMBE SET				
6 pieces ..	3/-	4/6	9/-	13/-
as above.				

MISS LANGLEY AND THE GREAT WESTERN POTTERY

The 1882 Newton Abbot Art Exhibition included a pair of vases, made at the Chudleigh Road Pottery, and decorated by a Miss Langley. In **Let's Collect Devon Pottery number three** we suggested that the Chudleigh Road Pottery was almost certainly The Great Western Pottery, later Candy Art Pottery, but who was 'Miss Langley'?

Howard Davies has searched the 1881 Census Returns and has found five 'Miss Langley's' who might be 'our' pottery artist.

Eliza E. Langley, aged 32
Frances M. Langley, aged 30
- these were sisters, the daughters of Charles Langley, who lived in Fore Street, Chudleigh

Sarah J. Langley, aged 60, living at Shute Hill, West Teignmouth, with her cousins:
Edith A. Langley, aged 36
Bertha M. Langley, aged 34
- Edith and Bertha, almost certainly sisters, had been born at Chudleigh.

None of these Miss Langley's is listed as having an occupation, and all appear to be 'comfortably off'. In the Victorian period it was quite common for ladies to occupy themselves by developing their artistic and creative skills – anything from needlework to music, painting and pottery decorating. So, perhaps it was one of these Miss Langley's who decorated the vases which attracted the attention of John Phillips, the owner of the Aller Vale Pottery and patron of the Cottage Art Schools.

If any readers can tell us more we'll be pleased to hear from you.

If you are interested in Candy Pottery you'll want to read:

CANDY ART POTTERY *by Ian Turner*

Published by the Hillian Press, The Old Brewery,
12 Church Street, Melbourne, Derbyshire DE73 1EJ

ISBN 0 9539751 0 X   Price £20

'MONKEY BUSINESS'

Although monkeys and chimpanzees have featured in ceramic art for at least 3,000 years it was Darwin's theories on evolution which brought them to the forefront of public attention in the late Victorian period. In his *Descent of Man,* published in 1871, Charles Darwin had suggested that all primates, including man, shared a common ancestor. In the public imagination this came to mean that monkeys were our ancestors. This idea spawned a wide variety of ceramics with monkey motifs, or models of monkeys; many companies made them – Wedgwood, Mintons, Burmantofts and the Devon potteries.

The Aller Vale Art Pottery illustrated two monkeys in its pattern books which date from the 1890's:

Shape 158

Monkey tobacco
shape 1514

On the left, the monkey holds a bowl, probably a sweet dish. On the right is a tobacco jar in the form of a monkey's head, wearing a jester's hat. Although these are in the pattern book, neither of them has been seen – unless any of our readers know otherwise!

The Watcombe Pottery made ashtrays with a monkey warming his (or her!) hands on a burning cigar butt. These were made in two sizes

– on a rectangular base, as shown in the photo, and on a smaller square base; they are made of white clay and date from the late 1890's. Some twenty years later the Devonmoor Art Pottery used a similar idea with a monkey squatting beside a bowl shaped ashtray. These were made in brown clay when the pottery first started production in 1922; later they were made in white clay using the same moulds.

Hart and Moist at Exeter made models of a sitting monkey sporting a very 'superior' expression! Some of these are inscribed *'Our ancestor'* down their backs – an obvious reference to Darwin. One of the most magnificent monkeys of all is the one made by C. H. Brannam in the 1890's; it is sitting beside an elaborately decorated bowl which houses an inkwell. A very rare item indeed. Of a later date is a small squatting monkey, wearing a bonnet (so obviously a 'she'!), made by William Baron; these were probably intended to be amusing novelties for children.

After World War I the craze for 'our ancestors' had run out of steam and few were made. The models are fun, though, and make an interesting collection for Devon pottery enthusiasts.

Photographs opposite:
Top, left: Devonmoor ashtray with squatting monkey. Inscribed inside the bowl: *'Who burned the tablecloth?*. **Right:** Watcombe ashtray, 21cms (8.5") wide, with monkey warming his hands on a cigar butt; made in the 1890's.
Middle, left to right: Hart and Moist model of a monkey with *'Our ancestor'* inscribed down his back, c.1903; Monkey inkwell, 23cms (9") wide, made by C. H. Brannam and dated 1893; small model of a monkey wearing a bonnet by William Baron.
Bottom row: ' Monkey business' of a different kind! Three 'loveable rogues' on a smuggling expedition. The two on the left are studying a map and have their oars and lamp at the ready; the one on the right is coming home with a chest full of 'booty'. These models were made by Alan Young (son of Will Young) in the 1980's.

NEW BOOK

North Devon Pottery *by Alison Grant*

Published by Edward Gaskell,
4 Market Street, Appledore, Devon, EX39 1PW

ISBN 189854677 – 0   Price £20

CANDY FIRE PLACE

A Candy fire place might be more 'at home' in a book for architects than pot collectors – but… this one's a miniature, as Bill Loram explains:

I bought this miniature Candy fire-place at an auction earlier this year. As it is such an unusual piece, I had high hopes the vendor would tell me it's history but, alas, it was sold by a man who had bought it at a car boot sale!

The fire-place is 37cms (14.5") across, 21.5cms (8.5") high, and 20cms (8") deep. It is a model of a 'Kenton' fireplace, which was 60" wide and 36" high; in a Candy catalogue published in the mid 1930's these retailed at £24. 10s. 0d. each.

This is the only miniature Candy fireplace I've ever seen. I asked Ian Turner (author of *Candy Art Pottery*) for his views and he suggests it could have been used at exhibitions (such as the Ideal Home Exhibition) to advertise Candy's wares. Has anyone else seen anything like this?